Hand Quilting

with Alex Anderson

Six Projects for Hand Quilters

C&T PUBLISHING

©1998 Alex Anderson
Illustrations ©1998 C&T Publishing

Developmental Editor: Liz Aneloski
Technical Editor: Joyce Engels Lytle
Copy Editor: Judith M. Moretz
Design Director: Diane Pedersen
Designer: Bobbi Sloan Design
Illustrator: Gretchen Schwarzenbach, GNS Graphics
Photography: Sharon Risedorph
Cover: Kathy Lee, Diane Pedersen, John Cram
Cover Photo taken at Ravenswood Historical site in Livermore, California, Livermore Area Recreation and Park District

Published by C&T Publishing, Inc., P.O. Box 1456, Lafayette, California 94549

Library of Congress Cataloging-in-Publication Data

Anderson, Alex (Alexandra)
    Hand quilting with Alex Anderson : six projects for hand quilters / Alex Anderson
            p.   cm.
    ISBN 1-57120-039-8
    1. Quilting. 2. Quilting—Patterns. 3. Patchwork—Patterns.
    I. Title
    TT835.A517   1998
    746.46—dc21
                                            97-31930
                                            CIP

C&T Publishing, Inc.
P.O. Box 1456
Lafayette, CA 94549
(800) 284-1114
http://www.ctpub.com
To request a catalog of fine books.

The Cotton Patch Mail Order
3405 Hall Lane, Dept. CTB
Lafayette, CA 94549
e-mail: cottonpa@aol.com
(800) 835-4418
(510) 283-7883
To request a catalog of quilting supplies.

Printed in Hong Kong

10 9 8 7 6 5 4 3

Contents

Introduction 3

Supplies 4
Fabric, Marking Tools, Batting, Needles, Thread, Thimbles, Frame or Hoop, Instructions for a Sawhorse Quilt Frame

Preparing to Quilt 9
Choosing Quilting Designs, Preparing Paper Quilting Templates, Marking the Quilting Designs, Layering the Quilt, Basting the Quilt, Placing the Quilt in a Hoop

The Quilting Stitch 13

Finishing the Quilt 21
Binding the Quilt, Labeling the Quilt

Projects 22
Wreath and Star Pillow   22
Bars Wallhanging   24
Center Diamond Wallhanging   26
One-Patch Wallhanging   28
Grapes and Pinwheels Wallhanging   30
Sawtooth Star Wallhanging   32

Quilting Design Patterns 35

ACKNOWLEDGMENTS

Thank you to:

The terrific people at C&T Publishing—your dedication to quality and continuous creative spirit is an ongoing inspiration to me. You are the BEST! Robert Kaufman Company, Inc. for producing an excellent product line, Kona™ Cotton—your fabric quilts like butter, and Elizabeth Phinder for your kindness—your generosity made the development of the quilts and this book a creative joy; All the quilters before us who have set standards of excellence that we all can learn from; The person unknown who taught me how to take my first stitches so many years ago; Kay for your beautiful roses and generous spirit, Linda Ballou for your friendship and attention to detail; Lee Ellen Cash for sharing the plans for making a sawhorse quilt frame, and last but not least, thank you to Mom and Dad, John, Joey, and Adair—I love you all.

Introduction

I love to hand quilt. My passion for hand quilting started about twenty years ago, when I picked up my first thimble. The hand quilting process and results cannot be matched in any other format. The satisfaction of sitting at a quilting frame in the middle of chaos (I have two teenagers), or alone, simply enjoying the silence and time to reflect, is a pleasure no quilter should skip. I love watching the quilt come to life as each little stitch is put in place.

But, do I always hand quilt? I wish the answer could be "yes," but the truth is, "no." It strictly depends on the fate of the quilt. Since I am fortunate to have quilting as my vocation, I now find that my quilts fall into two categories; working or heirloom quilts. My working quilts are often created for publications and need to be finished in a limited amount of time, or possibly it is a quilt that will be loved and used by a child. My heirloom quilts come under the category of quilting recreation, or quilts that are strictly made for the joy and love of the process, often resulting in show pieces. These are the quilts my kids will one day fight over. I think you know what I mean.

When I first started quilting, and to this day, I have always been intrigued by Amish quilts. Their strong, graphic, pieced tops coupled with beautiful quilting designs are enough to make even the strongest heart skip a beat. My first "real" quilting class was taught by a Mennonite woman in my area, Lucy Hilty. In her class we learned how to draw feathers, cables, and all those really neat quilting motifs. With this knowledge I made a classic Amish diamond quilt. This experience led me to an intense appreciation of hand quilting. I thank Lucy for opening my eyes to the world of beautiful, well-designed, traditional, hand quilted quilts.

I can remember many satisfying hours at the quilting frame putting in stitches, watching my pieced tops take form right before my eyes! It was almost as if I was breathing life right into them. If I had ten minutes to spare you could find me sitting at the quilting frame. I knew it was time to stop when my son Joey, then a little boy, would stand up under the quilt stretched on the frame, creating a head mountain. This little protest would make it impossible to quilt. My daughter Adair, then an infant, would wake from her afternoon nap demanding attention. Oh, when would I steal ten more minutes?

My father and I developed, and still have, a quilt frame business called Sladky Quilt frames. When we vend a show, people always stop by to watch me quilt. They are fascinated by the speed and ease of the process. (Through the process of hand quilting several dozen quilts during the first decade of my quilting career, I quickly developed the skill for creating little stitches.) What really surprises observers is that I can quilt in all directions using three different fingers: my middle, pointer, and thumb. With a short lesson, and a little practice, many people have learned to hand quilt in the same manner. Even my dad knows how to do it! Once you learn these simple techniques your life will be changed, forever! So let's get started.

To my Dad, who built my first quilt frame —

and to the Inghams, from whom

we stole the lumber.

Supplies

In hand quilting, the sky is the limit when it comes to tools. With so many tools available it's difficult to know where to start. I will share with you the products I use and why. When you understand the basic properties of the tools feel free to try other brands. What works for one person might not be the right choice for another. Before you know it you will understand what works best for you. But always remember you generally get what you pay for, with few exceptions.

Fabric

Always work with the best 100% cotton available. The quilts in this book were made using Kona Cotton solid-colored fabrics by Robert Kaufman Company, Inc.—the colors are wonderful and they needle beautifully. How a fabric needles refers to how easily the needle glides through the fabric— which enables you to get little stitches. I will often bring a quilting needle along to the quilt store to test the "quiltability" of the fabric (how it needles). I take a few passes through the cloth to determine how easily the needle slides through the fabric. If the fabric grabs at the needle or seems difficult to get through, put the fabric back on the shelf and pick another bolt. Avoid using cotton/polyester blends. While they might seem softer and therefore a more likely choice for ease of quilting, I have found the fibers "grab" the needle, making the quilting experience slow and frustrating. Be sure to choose fabrics carefully. I am always amazed at the diversity of fabrics that can exist under the same roof!

If you are using fancy quilting motifs, as we are in this book's projects, the more visually exciting the print of the fabric, the less your quilting designs will show. This is why I chose to use solid-colored fabrics. Let those cables and feathers spring forth!

Beware of "bargain" fabrics. Only the seasoned quiltmaker should partake in this type of purchase. Many times these "great deals" are fabrics with a lesser thread count (fewer threads per inch) which can cause the fabric to stretch or distort and wear out quickly. These fabrics can also be scattered with imperfections and flaws. When you hand quilt, many hours will be spent handling and working with the fabric. What a shame to have the fabric fall apart right before your eyes after many stitches have been lovingly put in.

Avoid using a bed sheet or decorator cloth for the top or the backing. The higher thread count (more threads per inch) makes it extremely difficult to hand quilt, because the needle will not slide between the threads easily.

There are different schools of thought as to whether you should prewash, or at least pretest, your fabric. My philosophy is, at a minimum you should test, but probably prewash, and here are my three reasons.

1. When the quilt is laundered, 100% cotton can shrink, causing puckers and distortion of the shape.

2. The darker color dyes have been known to migrate to the lighter fabrics in quilts. This defines the expression "heartbreak." Always prewash darks and lights separately.

3. Fabric is treated with chemicals, and I don't think it is healthy to breathe or handle these chemicals over an extended period of time. I have found myself wheezing when I decided to pass up prewashing.

If you choose not to prewash, test your fabric by cutting a two-inch square and putting it in boiling water. See if any color bleeds into the water. If it does, repeat the process. If the fabric continues to discharge color, throw it away (reds and purples are extremely suspect). It could ruin your quilt.

Take advantage of the wonderful quilt stores scattered across our planet. It is here you will get the best products available. Your time and your quilts deserve the best fabric available.

Marking Tools

I am frequently asked, "What do you mark with?" After gracefully trying to dodge the question (because there is no definitive answer), I usually recommend pre-marking fancy quilting motifs like the ones in this book using a silver Verithin™ pencil. For corrections or additions while quilting, I use a white charcoal pencil or white powder chalk. If you are using a colored marking product, always test it on the fabric you are using, to make sure the markings will come out. Sometimes the colors in the marking tools react to the finish on the cloth, resulting in permanent disaster. Quilting masking tape is ¼" wide and great for marking grid lines. Always read the instructions given for the different products. Avoid using a #2 lead pencil. The markings may not be able to be removed from the fabric.

Batting

The number one question I am asked when teaching and lecturing is, "What batting do you use?" Unfortunately, no one batting is the best choice for every project.

Basically, three types of fiber content are found in batting: cotton, polyester, and wool. Each type is appropriate for different looks and purposes. Here are some of the differences in a nutshell.

Cotton

Most old quilts have 100% cotton batting (with close inspection you might even see some cotton seeds). Although cotton batting is much more difficult to hand quilt, because the needle does not slide through the cotton as easily as through polyester or wool batting, it beards less than polyester. Bearding is when the batting migrates through the quilt top so you see little "tails" of fuzz on the quilt. This dis-

tracts from the look of the quilt. Bearding is an important issue when working with dark fabrics. Cotton provides a wonderful look, and the quilt will drape beautifully. Always read the instructions on the batting bag, since some cotton battings require prewashing. Cotton batting should be quilted heavily (your lines of quilting should be close together), generally every one to two inches, or the batting will pull apart and become lumpy. Imagine a bag of wet cotton balls!

Polyester

There are some wonderful polyester battings on the market. They are available in different lofts: low, medium, and high. The loft is the thickness of the batt. Low loft is wonderful for a highly pieced quilt (because of all the seam allowances you have to quilt through), or to achieve the flat, "drapey" look that cotton provides. Medium loft is just a little thicker, adding more body and providing more warmth. Stay away from high loft when hand quilting; it should be reserved for tied quilts. With polyester you don't have to quilt as heavily as with cotton; every two to three inches is fine.

Cotton/Polyester Blend

This type of batting is generally made of 80% cotton and 20% polyester. It has the look and feel of cotton but is almost as easy to hand quilt as polyester, and there is very little bearding. Always read the instructions on the batting bag, as some cotton/polyester blends require prewashing. This type of batting needs to be quilted every three inches or less.

Wool

There is nothing as wonderful as quilting on wool batting. Your needle will slide through like butter. Unfortunately, wool is very expensive. You might want to try using wool sometime, but maybe not for your first quilt.

Summary

Always make sure your batting is made by a reputable company. Inexpensive brands are often uneven in loft and are not properly treated. This is not a place to skimp. For your first experience, to date, I recommend either a light polyester batting or, if you just have to work with cotton, try a cotton/polyester blend. Always read the instructions on the batting bag, since some of the cottons and cotton/polyester blends require prewashing. The more you understand about the different principals of batting the better the decisions you will be able to make for your quilts. There is no one type of batting that is better than another; they all are used for different looks and needs.

For ease of needling Fairfield Low Loft®, Hobbs Poly Down®, and Mountain Mist Quilt Light® work quite nicely. The only exception is that if your quilt has a lot of solid black fabric you might want to use a cotton/polyester batting to reduce the bearding.

Some of these products only come in large sizes. If this is the case, you can use the pieces from one batt for several small projects by cutting it into smaller sections. Always feel free to ask your local quilt shop for guidance and to see samples. To learn more about this interesting subject matter I recommend you read *From Fiber to Fabric* by Harriet Hargrave (C&T Publishing).

Needles

Quilting needles are called betweens. They are sharp and short, and made specifically for hand quilting. At first they will seem too small to be real, but soon you will learn that the smaller the needle, the smaller the stitch. They are sized by number— the larger the number, the smaller the size of the needle. I recommend that you first start with size 8, then try 9, and so forth. Some quilters use size 12, but personally I can't thread them and they are too fragile for me. I use size 10.

If the needle gets sticky with oxidation from sweaty fingers or humidity, or gets bent, throw it away. Generally you will get what you pay for. Try different brands; they are all a little different.

Thread

There are threads made specifically for hand quilting, and they are available in a variety of wonderful colors. Quilting thread is a little heavier than regular sewing thread so there is no need to use beeswax on the thread. Some are made of 100% cotton and others have a polyester core with a cotton outside wrap. If your quilt is 100% cotton, I recommend using a 100% cotton thread. A polyester thread might cause the 100% cotton fabric to wear faster since polyester thread can cut the cotton fibers. If your quilt has many different types of fibers in it you might want to try a cotton covered polyester thread. Just as with needles, try different brands to find the one you like best.

For your first project, you might want to match your thread to the quilt so your stitches blend with the fabric. As you become more confident with your stitches, try using contrasting thread so the stitches show and become a design element. It just depends on the look you want for your quilt. It's also OK to use several colors of thread on the same quilt. The choice is yours.

Metallic threads give an interesting look (see border on the Sawtooth Star Wall-hanging, page 32). This type of thread is fragile to work with because it has a metallic wrap around the outside of a polyester or rayon core. If your piece of thread is too long or you tug your needle and thread aggressively, the outside metallic wrap will strip from the inner core. Sulky® has an interesting option called Sliver® Metallic thread. Sliver resembles a thin piece of colored Mylar® and is easier to work with than some other metallic threads. It looks a little thicker. To date, I prefer Sulky metallic or Sliver threads.

Thimbles

Wearing a thimble will feel awkward when you first start to quilt. In time it won't; trust me. A thimble is a must if you are going to learn the proper quilting stitch. The most important property of a good thimble is that it must have deep dimples. The thimble's job is to hold the eye of the needle as you rock it up and down through all three layers of the quilt to make the stitches. The thimble Grandma used for sewing will only cause frustration, because the needle will keep popping or sliding off the thimble due to the indentations being too shallow.

Make sure the thimble has a nice fit. It should be comfortable, but not so loose that it falls off when you gently shake your hand.

When you first start to hand quilt you will learn how you use the thimble in relationship to the needle—everyone is different. Which finger seems the most natural to wear the thimble: middle, pointer, thumb, or a combination? Do you work off the side or the end of the thimble? There are many considerations when choosing the right thimbles.

These answers come with a little practice and experimentation. After you determine how you work, you might want to invest in more expensive thimbles made specifically for your needs. There are thimbles with a little ridge around the top for people who work off the end. There are open-end thimbles for people with long fingernails. There are several different kinds of thimbles on the market now to choose from.

Your thimble is your most valuable tool.

Thimbles are a very personal choice, kind of like a pillow, and once you've found the perfect thimbles panic ensues if they are ever misplaced.

Classic metal thimble: indentations on both the sides and end

Open-end thimble: ridge at the end so the needle won't slide off under your fingernail

Thimble with a rim around the end: perfect for working off the end of the thimble

Frame or Hoop

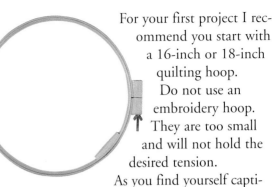

For your first project I recommend you start with a 16-inch or 18-inch quilting hoop.

Do not use an embroidery hoop. They are too small and will not hold the desired tension.

As you find yourself captivated with the process of hand quilting you will eventually want to invest in or build a frame. (See the following instructions to build a simple sawhorse frame.) A frame gives excellent tension control and keeps your quilt flat and square. It is much easier to get little stitches when the three layers are being held together evenly with the right tension. A frame also creates less stress on the quilt and the markings stay on longer. It is frustrating to mark an entire quilt top only to find the marking lines gone when you get to the edge of the quilt. You will know when it's time to invest in a frame. At that time, shop at quilt shows and quilt shops, and make sure it has the three following components: excellent tension control, stability, and ease of assembly. Only purchase a frame that you have seen in person or one that has been recommended by a fellow quilter. Last but not least, make sure it has a good warranty. This is a significant purchase that should last you a lifetime.

For your first project, stick to a hoop. Due to its portability, it is a tool you will use throughout your quilting career. We quilters like to travel, often with work in progress.

There is another technique called lap quilting. It is when you quilt without any tool holding the three layers taut. I strongly recommend that you DO NOT start with this technique. While you will be able to get smaller stitches right off the bat (no pun intended), the stitch is achieved through a completely different technique. I often meet people who started this way and find the transition to a hoop and frame nearly impossible. If you limit yourself in this way, large projects with intricate quilting designs will be difficult and cumbersome. Take the time to learn the correct quilting stitch. You will be forever grateful you took the time. Speed and excellence will be your reward.

Instructions for a Sawhorse Quilt Frame

The "It's Not Pretty, But It Works" frame is an inexpensive way to build your first frame. The materials cost less than $25.00 and it takes less than an hour to complete! I built my own sawhorses, which kept the price down. If you choose to purchase pre-made sawhorses, make sure the top bars are wood.

Materials

Two 30" high sawhorses
Two 2 x 2 boards the width of the quilt plus 12"
(for the projects in this book, use 42" boards)
Four 4½" x ⅜" screw eyes

Construction

1. Drill two ⅜" holes two inches from each end of the 2 x 2 boards in both directions.

2. Drill three ⅜" holes on each end of the top wooden bar of the sawhorses two inches apart, beginning two inches from each end, to insert the screw eye into.

That's it! Baste your quilt leaving three or four extra inches of backing on the top and bottom edges of the quilt. Thumbtack this extra backing onto the 2 x 2 boards. Roll equal amounts of the quilt on each board (like a roll of film that is half used). Position the boards on top of the sawhorses and drop the screw eyes through the 2 x 2 boards and into the sawhorses. Get the quilt as taut as possible.

Here's the real secret—Once the quilt is in position as tight as possible, push the quilt down in the center between the 2 x 2 boards across the entire width of the quilt. This will help to tightly pack the quilt around the boards. Then pull out the screw eyes and re-roll the boards to tighten the quilt again. Repeat this process until a flea could use it as a trampoline. Once the quilt is tightly wound on the frame, feel free to adjust the tension. I have found I can quilt much faster if the tension is slightly loose.

The beauty of this beginners' frame is that if you want to upgrade to a different frame, you have next year's Father's Day gift already purchased!

Tip: To keep sleepy cats from resting on your quilt, lay a sheet of aluminum foil over the quilt. The kitties will quickly find another place to snooze.

Preparing to Quilt

Choosing Quilting Designs

The quilting designs in this book are typical of the kind you might find on an Amish quilt. I have simplified them to fit the size and scale of the pillow and wallhanging projects that appear beginning on page 22. Feel free to mix and match them, using the quilting patterns that strike your fancy. For example, all the borders in this book are 5 inches wide, so any of the border patterns given will work quite nicely. Note that there are two sizes of square motifs. Use the appropriate size motif for each space. In addition, here are some general rules I use when deciding which quilting designs to use:

1. Fill the space. This is a rule we learned in kindergarten. If you have a 5-inch space use a 5-inch motif. A smaller motif will look skimpy.

2. Use an adequate amount of quilting. This alone can make or break the quilt.

3. Use an equal amount of quilting across the entire surface. If one area is left unquilted it will sag and look unbalanced.

4. It's OK to quilt over pieced units with a quilting design. Look at One-Patch Wallhanging on page 28 and Sawtooth Star Wallhanging on page 32 to see how the border is actually two different pieces of fabric quilted with one motif.

Marking Grids

Grids are a great way to fill an open area or to help accentuate a quilt design. If the area is small, like the alternate blocks of One-Patch Wallhanging (page 28), just mark the block from corner to corner, then find the center on the top, bottom, and sides of the block, make registration marks, and mark the grid.

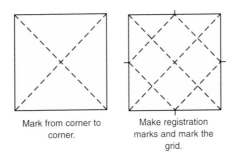

Mark from corner to corner.

Make registration marks and mark the grid.

If you would like the entire top to have a square grid on point (see Bars Wallhanging, page 24), there are a few ways to approach this. One way is to use the pieced units to determine where the registration marks for the grid will be and draw the lines to the marks. Once you have drawn the basic lines, you can add more lines in between the basic lines if you choose (see Sawtooth Star Wallhanging, page 32).

If your quilt has no determining pieced areas to mark from, first mark a line from corner to corner (this is for a square quilt). Then decide how far apart you want the grid lines, making sure the quilt measurement is evenly divisible by this number. Figure out the distance of this grid size at a 45 degree angle. Measure across the top, bottom, and sides of the quilt, making registration marks where the grid lines need to go. Then draw lines to connect the grid marks. The size of the grid you choose will be determined by the type of batting you are using (see Batting, page 5) and personal taste.

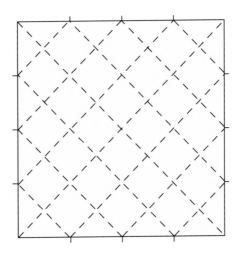

Make registration marks at equal distances around the quilt edge.

9

There are many ways to create grids. Be open to trying new techniques as you learn about them. Keeping these basic rules in mind, I look to quilts from the past for ideas and inspiration.

Stitching in the Ditch

Stitching in the ditch means quilting right next to the sewn seamline. You must determine the direction the seams are pressed and stitch on the opposite side of the seam. This helps avoid quilting through many layers of fabric. I like stitching in the ditch rather than stitching the traditional ¼" from the seamline, because stitching in the ditch keeps the sewn seamlines from visually popping up (see Grapes and Pinwheel Wallhanging, page 30).

Preparing Paper Quilting Templates

There are several different types of quilting templates available to quiltmakers. In this book we are using paper templates. Either trace the pattern with a Sharpie® felt tip pen onto a piece of translucent paper (typing paper will work, vellum is best) or photocopy the patterns from the book (if a little distortion occurs it's OK because quilting patterns, unlike piecing templates, are not an exact science). Due to the page size of this book, some of the quilting patterns will need to be "pieced" together. Cut out a piece of translucent paper that is approximately the desired finished size. Draw the unit as one motif, matching the dotted lines, or simply photocopy the quilting pattern parts and tape them together.

Marking the Quilting Designs

When marking a quilt (this is when you transfer the quilting design onto the pieced surface) pin the drawing to the underside of the quilt top. Marking must be done *before* you baste the quilt together (see Basting, page 12). Pin, avoiding where any drawn lines will be, and transfer only one pattern at a time.

When transferring the design from paper to fabric you need a light source. A light table works best. If you do not have access to one, tape your quilt top to a window—the sun will also work as a light source. A glass coffee table with a lamp under it will work as well. Another option is to buy ¼-inch-thick clear Plexiglas® (available at plastic and glass stores) and put it between two chairs with a lamp under it. My Plexiglas is 18" x 24". I have also heard of people opening up their dining room table and getting a piece of Plexiglas cut to the size of the opening. If you can't get your hands on a light table, first start with the window, but consider the above ideas for future quilts. The larger the quilt, the more difficult it is to use the window.

Transfer your pattern onto your quilt top using a silver Verithin pencil. I recommend you start with the interior patterns and work your way out to the borders. Don't worry if your markings are kind of sloppy. You can make adjustments with your white charcoal pencil as you hand quilt on your project.

Notice there are three kinds of borders given. First is a segment border (see the border on the Sawtooth Star Wallhanging, page 32). It is a repeat of an independent pattern. This type of motif can be transferred onto the border section by section or as a complete unit. To transfer as a complete unit, cut a piece of translucent paper the finished size of the border of one side of the quilt. Trace and repeat the pattern to fill the space on the translucent paper. Pin this paper quilting template to the underside of the quilt top and mark the quilting design onto the quilt top. Sometimes it is easier to have the individual units drawn on one piece of paper as a complete unit. This avoids any spacing problems that might occur.

Transfer motif section by section or as a complete unit.

Second, there is a continuous border pattern (see the single feather border on the One-Patch Wallhanging, page 28). Cut a piece of paper the finished size of the border and trace the pattern, then transfer onto the quilt top.

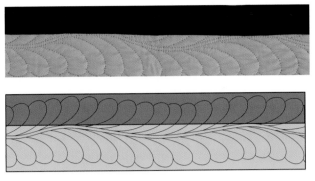

Transfer motif as one continuous pattern.

Third, is a turned corner border (see the grapevine border on the Grapes and Pinwheels Wallhanging, page 30, and Center Diamond Wallhanging, page 26). While this border may look a little more complicated, it is really the easiest pattern of all, because you only have to draw one eighth of the border. Trace the pattern onto translucent paper. Starting with the diagonal edge, pin the pattern to the desired section of the quilt, making sure the corner lines up at a 45-degree angle, and transfer onto the quilt top. Then flip the pattern and transfer to the other edge. The design will automatically turn the corner of the quilt.

Transfer motif section by section.

That's all there is to it. Feel free to mix and match the patterns given in this book, or quilting designs from elsewhere. This is how your quilt will have your name and individual spirit stitched right on it.

Layering the Quilt

All the projects in this book are under 42 inches wide (the regular width of 100% cotton quilting fabric). This eliminates having to piece the backing together. Purchase one yard of fabric for the backing. Feel free to use a jazzy looking fabric. Not only will it surprise those who look at the back, but it will help to hide inconsistent stitches. Make sure your backing is at least three to four inches larger than the pieced top on each side. The extra fabric will come in handy when you are quilting close to the edges of your quilt. The excess backing fabric gives the hoop something to hold and keeps the edges of your quilt from stretching. Press the backing fabric before layering.

Layer your project either on a non-scratchable table top (check out your local church or quilt store) or on a non-loop carpet. First you must either tape down (table top) or pin using T-pins (carpet) the quilt backing wrong side up, working from the center of each side to the corners. Keep the fabric grain straight and stretch the backing taut, but not too tight. No bubbles or ripples are acceptable, or you will have folds and tucks on the back of your finished quilt.

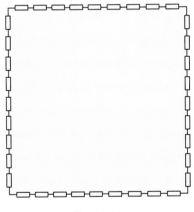

Tape backing.

Carefully unroll the batting and smooth it onto the backing. Trim the batting to about two inches larger than the quilt top on all sides. Center and smooth your pressed quilt top onto the batting right side up.

Basting the Quilt

Baste the quilt together to hold the layers in place during quilting. Knot one end of regular sewing thread and take large stitches through all three layers. Never use colored thread when basting—the dye might migrate onto the fabric. I like to baste in a grid pattern, about every four inches working from the center out to the edges. This gives an even amount of basting across the entire surface. Never skimp on this part of the process, it will only cause problems down the road, since your quilt can shift and move during the quilting process.

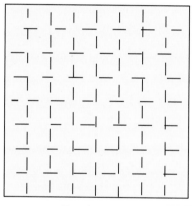

Baste in a grid.

Placing the Quilt in a Hoop

When working on a hoop, always work from the center of the quilt out to the edges to avoid puckers and folds in the quilt layers. To position the quilt in your hoop, loosen the screw of the hoop. Slide the smaller ring underneath the center of the quilt and place the larger ring (the one with the screw) on top of the quilt. Clamp the ring together and partially tighten the screw. Make sure the backing and top are equally smooth and stretched. Next, press your hand down in the middle of the hoop to loosen the tension, while keeping the quilt top and back equally taut. Tighten the screw all the way. Now the three layers can be manipulated easily.

Remove the hoop from the quilt between quilting sessions to avoid any stretching or distortion that may occur by leaving the hoop on the quilt for extended periods of time.

If you are using a frame rather than a hoop, refer to page 8 or your quilting frame manufacturer's instructions to learn how to attach your quilt to the frame.

Tricks:

1. Use the bowl end of a spoon to pick up the tip of the needle as it comes up through all the layers.

2. Don't bother knotting the other end of the thread. When it's time to remove the basting you can just give the knotted end of the thread a tug and it will pull out.

The Quilting Stitch

The quilting stitch is unlike any other sewing stitch, although it looks just like a simple running stitch. Whether you are left- or right-handed it is really quite easy to achieve with just a little practice. (I myself am a lefty.)

The stitch is created using a rocking motion while the thimble pushes the needle through all three layers of the quilt. This stitch requires three important fingers on your two hands all working in unison. On the top of the quilt (using the hand you write with), you will use your thimble finger and thumb. Under the quilt you will use either the pointer finger or middle finger of your other hand. All three fingers work together manipulating the needle through the hills and valleys your fingers create. Let's break it down into little steps.

Thread your needle. Tie a single knot about 18 inches down the length of the thread (never any longer to avoid tangling) and then snip off the thread from the spool. This will keep the "wrap" of the thread going in the right direction, resulting in less tangling.

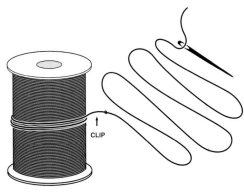

Thread, knot, and clip.

Insert your needle into the quilt top and batting (not into the backing) an inch away from where you want to start quilting, and bring the needle up to the spot where you want to start quilting. Gently pull the thread until the knot "pops" in between the three layers. This is called burying the knot.

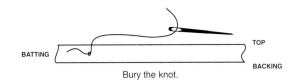

Bury the knot.

You must identify which finger you want to wear the thimble on. I wear the thimble on my pointer finger. Most quilters want to try their middle finger first, but either finger is fine. Try both ways to see which one is most comfortable.

Your next decision is whether you are going to use the end or the side of the thimble to push the needle. This will determine what type of thimble you will need (see Thimbles, page 7). I find that most middle-finger quilters seem to use the end of the thimble, and pointer-finger quilters want to work off the side. I work off the side of the thimble. Again, experiment and see what works for you. At best, it will all feel odd at first.

Put the hand without the thimble under the quilt with your pointer or middle finger (whichever is more comfortable) where the first stitch will be taken. Push up on the quilt, creating a "hill" into which the first stitch will be taken.

If you are right-handed refer to the photographs on pages 14, 15, and 16 and follow the step-by-step instructions.

If you are left-handed refer to the photographs on pages 17, 18, and 19 and follow the step-by-step instructions.

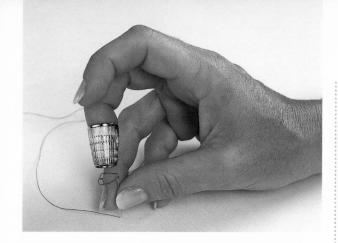

1. Place the hand with the thimble on top of the quilt. Hold the needle straight up and down between the thumb and ring finger.

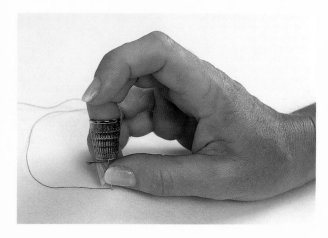

2. With the hand in a "C" position, insert the needle straight up and down into the quilt where the hill has been created by your finger underneath.

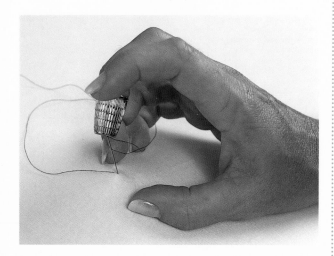

3. Release your fingers from the needle.

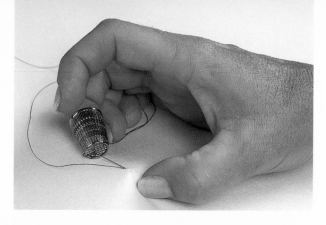

4. When you feel the prick of the needle you will do two things at once. Pivot the needle tip back up, using a dimple on the thimble to hold the needle. Push down with your thumb in front of the hill where the stitch is about to be taken. The needle should now be flat against the quilt. This will force the tip of the needle through the top of the hill, creating the first stitch.

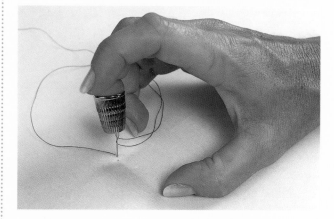

5. When you see the tip of the needle come through the hill, immediately move the finger under the quilt away. Pivot the blunt end of the needle back up perpendicular to the quilt, forcing the tip down into the valley. This needle motion is about a 90-degree movement. As soon as you prick your finger under the quilt (Yikes!, but not enough to draw blood), repeat the process.

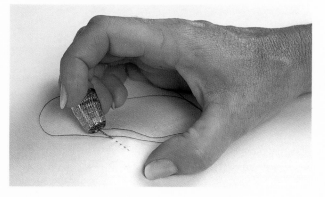

6. This motion is called the rocking stitch. Try to gather two or three stitches at a time onto your needle. Pull on the needle and thread until the thread is taut. Proceed to page 15.

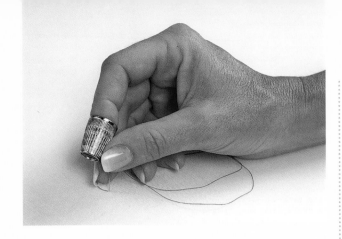

1. Place the hand with the thimble on top of the quilt. Hold the needle straight up and down between the thumb and middle finger.

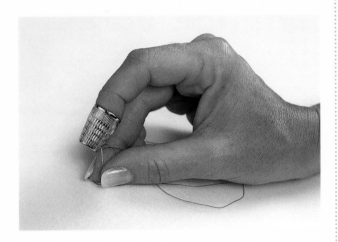

2. With the hand in a "C" position, insert the needle straight up and down into the quilt where the hill has been created by your finger underneath.

3. Release your fingers from the needle.

4. When you feel the prick of the needle you will do two things at once. Pivot the needle tip back up, using a dimple on the thimble to hold the needle. Push down with your thumb in front of the hill where the stitch is about to be taken. The needle should now be flat against the quilt. This will force the tip of the needle through the top of the hill, creating the first stitch.

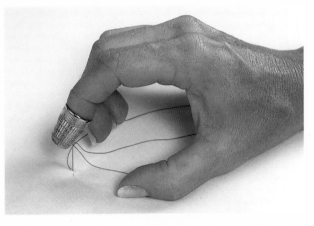

5. When you see the tip of the needle come through the hill, immediately move the finger under the quilt away. Pivot the blunt end of the needle back up perpendicular to the quilt forcing the tip down into the valley. This needle motion is about a 90-degree movement. As soon as you prick your finger under the quilt (Yikes!, but not enough to draw blood), repeat the process.

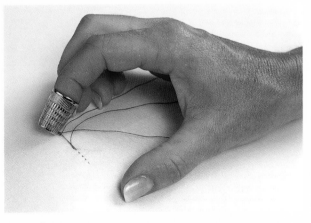

6. This motion is called the rocking stitch. Try to gather two or three stitches at a time onto your needle. Pull on the needle and thread until the thread is taut. Proceed to page 16.

Once you become confident with this stitch it's time to learn how to quilt away from yourself using a thimble on your thumb. It is exactly the same process, only in a different direction. Many people, like myself, prefer this way of quilting because the thumb is a much stronger finger, resulting in faster stitching. Also, if your hand gets weary from quilting in one direction it is nice to be able to get relief by going in another direction. Last but not least, it makes quilting feathers and grapes a snap!

First you will need a larger thimble that fits comfortably on your thumb. When you use the thumb you will use the side of the thimble to hold your needle, not the end.

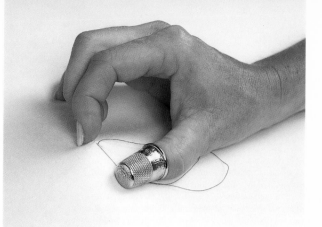

3. Rock the blunt end back, forcing the needle parallel to the quilt. Push down in front of the hill, with your top hand pointer finger, where the first stitch will be taken. Keep your hand in a "C" position.

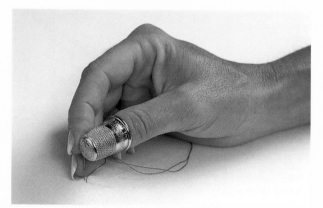

1. Hold the needle straight up and down between the thimble finger and your pointer and middle fingers. At first, it might seem odd to handle the needle with a thimble on your thumb, but you will be amazed how quickly you get used to it. Insert the needle into the quilt top straight up and down, pricking your underneath finger.

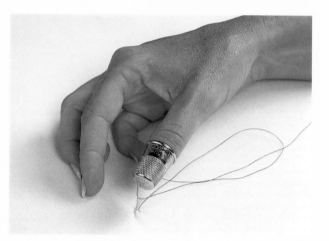

4. As soon as you see the tip of the needle come through the hill immediately move the finger under the quilt away. Pivot the blunt end of the needle back up perpendicular to the quilt forcing the tip down. This needle motion is about a 90-degree movement.

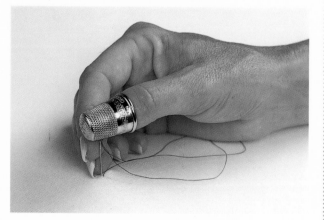

2. As soon as you feel the tip of the needle prick the underneath finger, roll the thimble to the top of the needle.

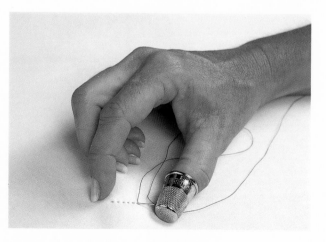

5. As soon as you prick your finger under the quilt, repeat the process above. Pull on the needle and thread until the thread is taut. Proceed to page 20.

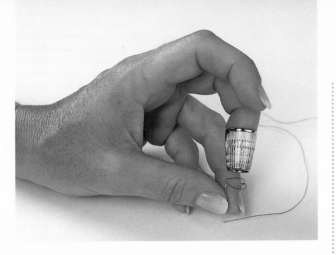

1. Place the hand with the thimble on top of the quilt. Hold the needle straight up and down between the thumb and ring finger.

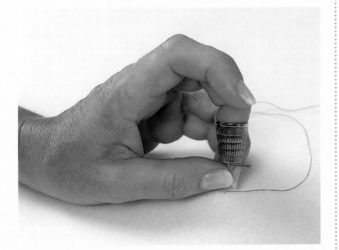

2. With the hand in a "C" position, insert the needle straight up and down into the quilt where the hill has been created by your finger underneath.

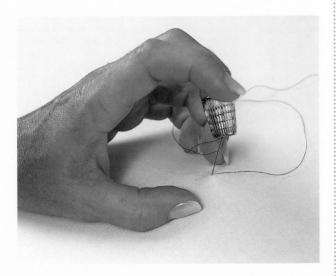

3. Release your fingers from the needle.

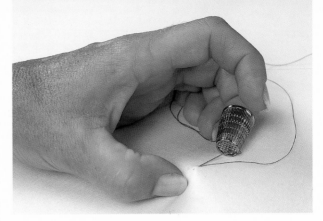

4. When you feel the prick of the needle you will do two things at once. Pivot the needle tip back up, using a dimple on the thimble to hold the needle. Push down with your thumb in front of the hill where the stitch is about to be taken. The needle should now be flat against the quilt. This will force the tip of the needle through the top of the hill creating the first stitch.

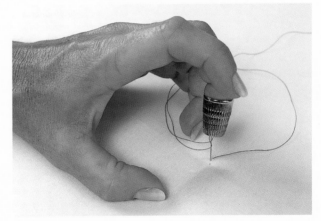

5. When you see the tip of the needle come through the hill, immediately move the finger under the quilt away. Pivot the blunt end of the needle back up perpendicular to the quilt, forcing the tip down into the valley. This needle motion is about a 90-degree movement. As soon as you prick your finger under the quilt (Yikes!, but not enough to draw blood), repeat the process.

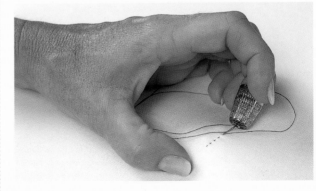

6. This motion is called the rocking stitch. Try to gather two or three stitches at a time onto your needle. Pull on the needle and thread until the thread is taut. Proceed to page 18.

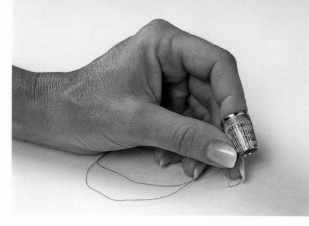

1. Place the hand with the thimble on top of the quilt. Hold the needle straight up and down between the thumb and middle finger.

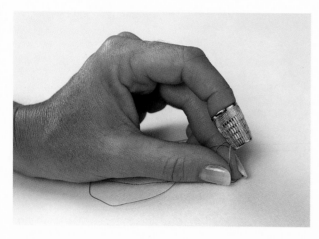

2. With the hand in a "C" position, insert the needle straight up and down into the quilt where the hill has been created by your finger underneath.

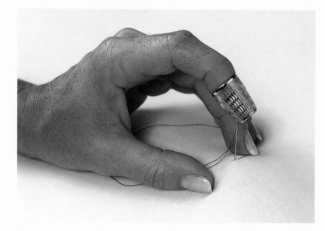

3. Release your fingers from the needle.

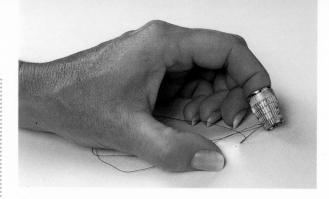

4. When you feel the prick of the needle you will do two things at once. Pivot the needle tip back up, using a dimple on the thimble to hold the needle. Push down with your thumb in front of the hill where the stitch is about to be taken. The needle should now be flat against the quilt. This will force the tip of the needle through the top of the hill, creating the first stitch.

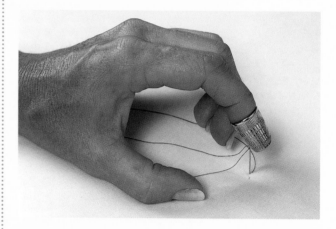

5. When you see the tip of the needle come through the hill, immediately move the finger under the quilt away. Pivot the blunt end of the needle back up perpendicular to the quilt, forcing the tip down into the valley. This needle motion is about a 90-degree movement. As soon as you prick your finger under the quilt (Yikes!, but not enough to draw blood), repeat the process.

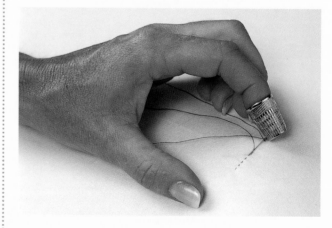

6. This motion is called the rocking stitch. Try to gather two or three stitches at a time onto your needle. Pull on the needle and thread until the thread is taut. Proceed to page 19.

Once you become confident with this stitch it's time to learn how to quilt away from yourself using a thimble on your thumb. It is exactly the same process, only in a different direction. Many people, like myself, prefer this way of quilting because the thumb is a much stronger finger, resulting in faster stitching. Also, if your hand gets weary from quilting in one direction it is nice to be able to get relief by going in another direction. Last but not least, it makes quilting feathers and grapes a snap!

First you will need a larger thimble that fits comfortably on your thumb. When you use the thumb you will use the side of the thimble to hold your needle, not the end.

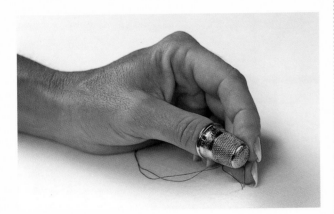

1. Hold the needle straight up and down between the thimble finger and your pointer and middle fingers. At first it might seem odd to handle the needle with a thimble on your thumb, but you will be amazed how quickly you get used to it. Insert the needle into the quilt top straight up and down, pricking your underneath finger.

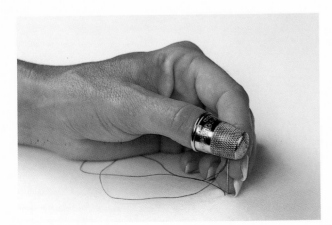

2. As soon as you feel the tip of the needle prick the underneath finger, roll the thimble to the top of the needle.

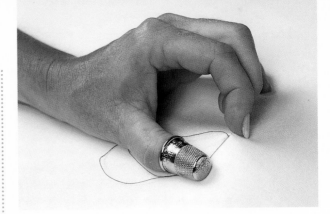

3. Rock the blunt end back, forcing the needle parallel to the quilt. Push down in front of the hill, with your top hand pointer finger, where the first stitch will be taken. Keep your hand in a "C" position.

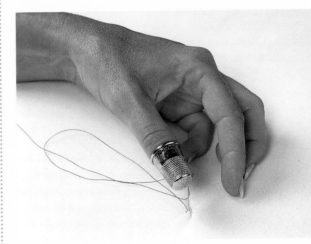

4. As soon as you see the tip of the needle come through the hill, immediately move the finger under the quilt away. Pivot the blunt end of the needle back up perpendicular to the quilt, forcing the tip down. This needle motion is about a 90-degree movement.

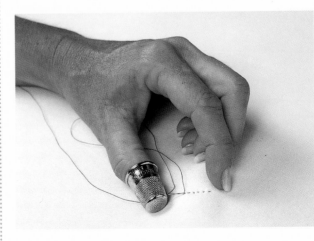

5. As soon as you prick your finger under the quilt, repeat the process above. Pull on the needle and thread until the thread is taut. Proceed to page 20.

With experience you will be able to get more than two or three stitches onto your needle, but try not to load up more than half of your needle with stitches. If you do, the needle can get stuck in the quilt, slowing down the entire process. At first, hand quilting might feel a little awkward, maybe even impossible, but remember, with a little practice and patience it will become second nature—kind of like riding a bike.

When quilting tight curves such as feathers and grapes, take only two or three stitches on the needle at a time, then reposition the needle. (This is how I learned to quilt in all directions.)

When you come to the end of your thread, tie a single knot close to the quilt surface. Put the needle into the same hole the thread is coming out of through the top and batting, and back through the quilt top. Pull gently on the thread, burying the knot between the three layers. Some people like to take a little back stitch for extra insurance that their stitches won't come out. Pull the remaining end of the thread up and carefully snip off the end.

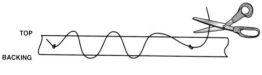

Bury the knot.

Tips

• Don't worry about the size of your stitches. Just try for a consistent stitch length. Counting the stitches on top, my first stitches were two to the inch! But remember, the smaller the "hill" the smaller your stitches will be.

• Don't pick out poor stitches as you go along. This takes away from valuable learning time. When the quilt is complete, feel free to locate those unsightly stitches and redo them; I promise it won't be worth your time.

• You don't have to end the thread whenever you move from one motif section to the next. If the distance between motifs is less than two needle lengths, consider "walking the needle." In the direction you want to move, insert the needle between the pieced top and quilt backing. Push the needle half of the way so the tip of the needle is between the top and backing of the quilt. Bring the tip of the needle halfway up through the top of the quilt.

Grab the tip of the needle and pivot the eye of the needle (which is still between the top and backing of the quilt). Push the needle back down into the quilt, continuing in the desired direction, leading with the eye of the needle. When you get to the desired location push the eye of the needle up through the top surface of the quilt. It will pierce the fabric just fine.

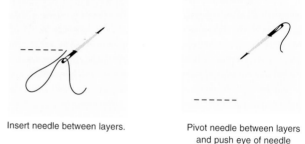

Insert needle between layers.

Pivot needle between layers and push eye of needle through

• If your first stitch is always bigger than the rest, try inserting your needle tilted a little bit more forward than straight up and down, or consider taking a backstitch to "cheat" the look.

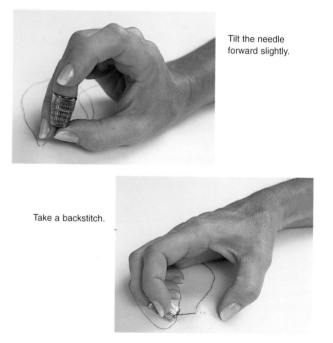

Tilt the needle forward slightly.

Take a backstitch.

• If there are several layers of fabric to stitch through, making the rocking stitch impossible, try taking one stitch at a time. Pass the needle through the top of the quilt to the bottom side of the quilt, pull the needle so the thread is taut, then push the needle back up through the quilt to the top and pull the thread taut. This is called the stab stitch.

Binding the Quilt

Trim batting and backing even with the quilt top.

1. Cut four strips of fabric 2¼" by the width (42"). Measure across the middle of the quilt and trim the binding strips to that measurement plus 1". Fold in half lengthwise and press.

2. On the top edge of the quilt, line up the raw edges of the binding with the raw edge of the quilt. Let the binding extend ½" past the corners of the quilt. Do this on the top and bottom of the quilt. Stitch.

3. Bring the folded edge of the binding over the raw edge of the quilt and slip stitch the binding to the back side of the quilt. Trim the ends even with the edge of the quilt as shown.

4. With the remaining two strips, fold in ½" on each end of the strip for a finished edge. Sew the binding strips on, bring the folded edge of the binding to the back side of the quilt, and slip stitch in place.

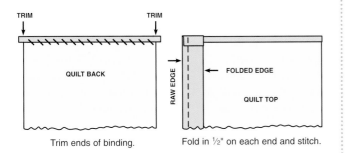

Trim ends of binding.   Fold in ½" on each end and stitch.

Labeling the Quilt

When hand quilting, the process usually includes an extended period of time, so I think it is fun to not only date and sign each quilt, but to include some current family history. Then, when I visit my quilts periodically, I am reminded of the time during which the quilt was created.

I usually mark directly on the back of the quilt with a permanent felt tip pen, however, you can create your own labels from unused quilt blocks or purchase pre-made labels to sew on the back of the quilt. It doesn't matter how you do it, the important thing is to "just do it!" You will be happy you did years from now when you reflect on the time and memories when you lovingly put in all those tiny stitches.

R$_X$ for Quilters—Simple First Aid Tips

• For instant relief of a poked finger try a drop of New Skin® in the offended area. Like magic a single drop fills in the hole and thirty seconds later it's time to quilt. New Skin is a liquid bandage available from your local drug store.

• For long-term healing rub Bag Balm® into your fingers at bedtime. It is a cow udder cream that provides long-term care for your fingers. It is available at animal feed or quilt stores and through quilting magazines by mail order.

• If you bleed on your quilt (sorry, but occasionally it does happen), instantly rub some of your own saliva on the blood. The enzymes will help remove the stain.

Summary

The first time I tried to hand quilt my hands suddenly had ten thumbs! My friend Wendy Grande picked up the thimble and took to quilting like a duck to water. I could not make heads or tails of the process, and today it is second nature. You will find yourself in one category or the other, but the main thing is do not give up; with just a little practice you too will be a hand quilter for life and loving every minute of it!

As I mentioned in the introduction, my first experience with hand quilting was to make a full-size Amish quilt. So much was learned through this process that I would like you to experience a similar journey. Because hand quilting creates a time commitment (although it's really not as time consuming as you think), let's postpone the bed-size quilt until you have completed one of these simple projects. I want you to enjoy the process, not to feel as if you have just signed your life away. I quilted each of these projects in less than ten hours. There are five simple wallhanging patterns for you to choose from, as well as a pillow. The bar and diamond wallhangings are very traditional and typical of the Amish style, while the others have a contemporary feeling. Through the creation of your quilt you will learn all the important details of hand quilting: everything from what type of designs are appropriate, to transferring designs onto the top, all the way to perfecting your stitch. Choose one of the five pieced quilt projects, or simply start with the pillow, then decide which quilting designs strike your fancy. I know that through the creation of one of these projects you too will become intrigued with the process of hand quilting. You will appreciate the joy of putting in the last stitch, knowing generations to come will enjoy your project!

Wreath and Star Pillow

Wreath and Star Pillow, 13½" x 13½", quilted with feathered wreath (page 35) and eight-pointed star (page 35)

Fabric Requirements

White fabric: 1¼ yards for the quilted pillow top, quilt backing, pillow back, and ruffle

Batting: 20" x 20"

Pillow form: 14" x 14"

White quilting thread

Cutting

Cut an 18" x 42" piece of fabric. Cut in half down the center fold for two pieces of fabric measuring 18" x 21" for the quilted pillow top and quilt backing.

Cut two 10" x 15" rectangles for the pillow back.

Cut two strips 8" x 42" (width of fabric) for the ruffle.

Instructions

1. Center and transfer the quilting design onto the pillow top (see Marking the Quilting Designs beginning on page 10).

2. Layer the backing, batting, and top, and put it into the hoop. Don't worry about basting the three layers together. Due to the size of this project it is not necessary.

3. Quilt (see The Quilting Stitch beginning on page 13).

CONSTRUCTION OF PILLOW

4. Trim the quilted pillow top to 14¼". This will give the pillow a tight fit.

5. For the ruffle: Sew the two 8"-wide strips into a continuous circle. Press the seams open. With wrong sides together, fold the circular strip in half lengthwise. Now your ruffle is only 4" wide.

6. Stitch two or three lines of gathering stitches on the raw edge of the ruffle.

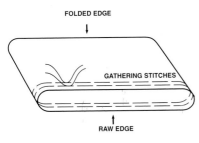

Stitch lines of gathering stitches.

7. Fold into quarters and place marks at the folds. These marks will help you evenly distribute the ruffle around the edge of the pillow.

8. Gather and pin to the pillow top matching each mark to a corner of the pillow top.

9. Using a large stitch, baste the ruffle in place using a ⅜" seam allowance.

Baste ruffle.

PREPARING A TWO-PIECE BACKING

10. Press under ¼" along one 15" edge of each backing piece. Press under another ¼" and top-stitch this edge.

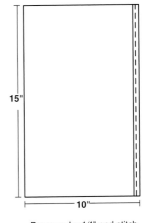

Press under 1/4" and stitch.

11. Overlap the two pieces, with the folded edges in the center, to create a 15" square.

12. With right sides together pin the pillow top and back together. (Note that the back is a little larger than the top for ease of construction.)

13. Using a ½" seam allowance sew around all four edges, easing in the extra back fabric.

14. Turn inside out and remove any unwanted gathering or basting stitches.

15. Insert the pillow form. For tight pillow corners, little balls of additional batting can be stuffed into the four corners.

Bars Wallhanging

Bars Wallhanging, 31" x 31", reproduction of a typical Amish, Lancaster County, PA, bars quilt, quilted with cable (page 40), crosshatch grid (page 9), and Baptist fans (page 40) for the border

Fabric Requirements

Blue: ¼ yard for the inner border

Gray: ⅞ yard for the bars and outer border

Red: ½ yard for the bars and border corners

Backing: 1 yard

Binding: ⅓ yard

Batting: 35" x 35"

Black quilting thread

Cutting

Red: Cut four 3½" x 21½" strips for the bars.
Cut four 4½" squares for the border corners.

Gray: Cut three 3½" x 21½" strips for the bars.
Cut four 4½" x 23½" strips for the outer border.

Blue: Cut two 1½" x 21½" strips.
Cut two 1½" x 23½" strips.

Piecing and Pressing

Use ¼" seam allowance. Press the direction the arrows indicate.

1. Sew the four red and three 3½" wide gray strips together, alternating the colors, with red on the two outside ends. Press.

2. Sew the two 21½" blue inner borders on the top and bottom of the bars. Press.

3. Sew the two 23½" blue inner borders onto the sides of the bars. Press.

4. Sew the four 4½" red squares onto both ends of two 4½"-wide gray outer borders. Press.

5. Sew the 4½"-wide gray side outer borders (without the red squares) onto the center section and press. Then sew on the top and bottom outer borders (with the red squares). Press.

Quilting design placement

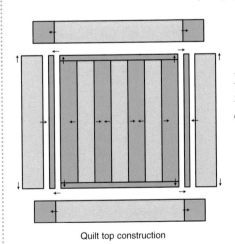

Quilt top construction

Easy as that! Now it's time to mark the top, layer, baste, and quilt.

ALTERNATE COLOR SCHEMES

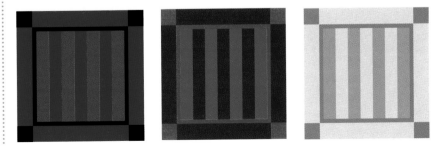

25

Center Diamond Wallhanging

Center Diamond Wallhanging, 30" x 30", typical Amish, Lancaster County, PA, center diamond quilt, quilted with feathered wreath (page 35), eight-pointed star (page 35) in the center, tulips (page 36), chain, continuous border (page 37), and a turned-corner feather, noncontinuous border (page 39)

Fabric Requirements

Pink: ⅜ yard for the center diamond and border corners

Blue: ⅓ yard for the corner triangles

Green: ⅛ yard for the inner border

Purple: ⅓ yard for the outer border

Backing: 1 yard

Binding: ⅓ yard

Batting: 34" x 34"

Black quilting thread

Cutting

Pink: Cut one 12½" square for the center diamond.

Cut four 2" squares for the inner border corners.

Cut four 5½" squares for the outer border corners.

Blue: Cut two 9⅜" squares, then cut diagonally once.

Green: Cut four 2" x 17½" strips.

Purple: Cut four 5½" x 20½" strips.

Piecing and Pressing

Use ¼" seam allowance. Press the direction the arrows indicate.

1. Sew the center unit in the order indicated. Press.

2. Sew the four 2" squares onto both ends of two inner borders. These will be the top and bottom inner borders. Press.

3. Sew the four 5½" squares onto both ends of two outer borders. These will be the top and bottom outer borders. Press.

4. Sew the inner side borders on the quilt top and press. Then sew on the inner top and bottom borders. Press.

5. Repeat Step 4 to add the outer borders.

Easy as that! Now it's time to mark the top, layer, baste, and quilt.

Quilting design placement

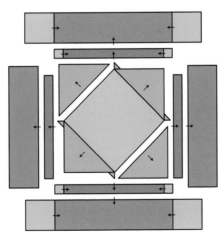

Quilt top construction

ALTERNATE COLOR SCHEMES

27

One-Patch Wallhanging

One-Patch Wallhanging, 30" x 30", twenty-five 4" one-patch blocks, quilted with simple flower (page 36) and simple grid (page 9), single feather border (page 37), with baskets (page 36) in the corners

Fabric Requirements

Assorted solid fabrics: ½ yard total for the twenty-five 4" blocks. (You may choose to include 4" blocks made from the leftover border fabrics for continuity.)

Black: ⅓ yard for inner border

Pink: ½ yard for outer border

Blue: ¼ yard for border corners

Backing: 1 yard

Binding: ⅓ yard

Batting: 34" x 34"

Black quilting thread

Cutting

Assorted solid fabrics: Cut twenty-five 4½" squares.

Black: Cut four 2½" x 20½" strips.

Pink: Cut four 3½" x 20½" strips.

Blue: Cut four 5½" squares.

Piecing and Pressing

Use ¼" seam allowance. Press the direction the arrows indicate.

1. Arrange and sew the twenty-five blocks in five rows of five squares each. Press.

2. Sew the five rows together. Press.

3. For all four borders, sew the black borders to the pink borders lengthwise. Press.

4. Sew the four 5½" blue squares onto both ends of two pieced borders. Press. These will be the top and bottom borders.

5. Sew the side borders on the quilt top and press. Then sew on the top and bottom borders. Press.

Easy as that! Now it's time to mark the top, layer, baste, and quilt.

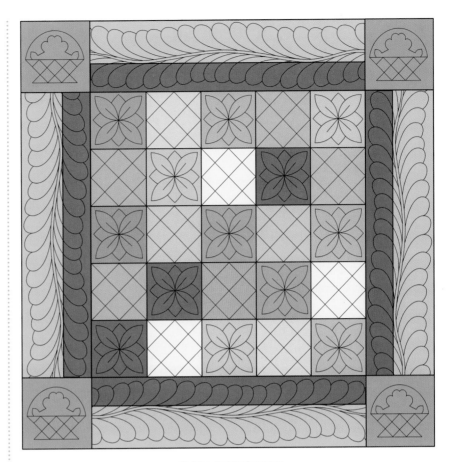

Quilting design placement

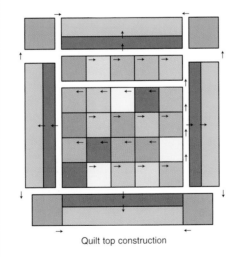

Quilt top construction

ALTERNATE COLOR SCHEMES

29

Grapes and Pinwheels Wallhanging

Grapes and Pinwheels Wallhanging, 30" x 30", sixteen 3½" pinwheels set on point, quilted with grape leaves (page 37), stitching in the ditch (page 10), a simple grid (page 9), and a continuous grapevine border (page 38)

Fabric Requirements

Light Pastels: a total of ¼ yard for the pinwheels

Medium Pastels: a total of ¼ yard for the pinwheels

White: ⅛ yard for the background

Light blue: ¼ yard for the background

Yellow: ¼ yard for the inner border

Green: ½ yard for the outer border

Backing: 1 yard

Binding: ⅓ yard

Batting: 33" x 33"

White quilting thread

Cutting

For one 3½" (finished) pinwheel:

Light Pastels: Cut two light 2⅝" squares, then cut in half diagonally.

Medium Pastels: Cut two medium 2⅝" squares, then cut in half diagonally.

Repeat for a total of sixteen blocks.

White: Cut nine 4" squares.

Light Blue: Cut three 6¼" squares, then cut in half diagonally twice. Cut two 3⅜" squares, then cut in half diagonally.

Yellow: Cut two 2" x 20½" strips. Cut two 2" x 23½" strips.

Green: Cut two 4" x 23½" strips. Cut two 4" x 30½" strips.

Piecing and Pressing

Use ¼" seam allowance. Press the direction the arrows indicate.

3½" PINWHEELS

1. Sew one light half-square triangle to one medium half-square triangle. Repeat three more times in the same color combination. Press.

Sew one light and one medium triangle together.

2. Sew the four squares to make a pinwheel, press.

Repeat Steps 1 and 2 until you have all sixteen pinwheels sewn.

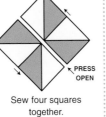
PRESS OPEN
Sew four squares together.

3. Lay out your blocks as shown. Note that they are set on point with the alternate white background squares.

4. Join the blocks, the white background squares, and the side and corner light blue triangles in diagonal rows. Press.

5. Sew on the 20½" yellow borders to the sides and then the 23½" yellow borders to the top and bottom. Press.

6. Repeat with the outer green borders, attaching the 23½" borders to the sides and the 30½" borders to the top and bottom. Press.

Easy as that! Now it's time to mark the top, layer, baste, and quilt.

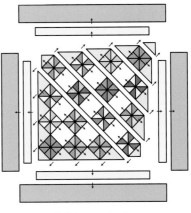
Quilt top construction

Quilting design placement

ALTERNATE COLOR SCHEMES

Sawtooth Star Wallhanging

Sawtooth Star Wallhanging, 28" x 28", five 6" sawtooth stars and four 6" nine-patches,
quilted with an overall diagonal grid (page 9) and segmented leaf border (page 35)

Fabric Requirements

Blue: ⅞ yard for the stars and outer border

Yellow: ½ yard for the nine-patches and inner border

White: ½ yard for the stars and nine-patches

Backing: 1 yard

Binding: ⅓ yard

Batting: 32" x 32"

White quilting thread and Sulky Sliver blue metallic thread

Cutting

Blue: Cut five 3½" squares for the stars (1S).

Cut twenty 2⅜" squares, then cut in half diagonally for the stars (2S).

Cut two 3½" x 22½" strips for the outer border.

Cut two 3½" x 28½" strips for the outer border.

Yellow: Cut three 2½" strips for the nine-patches.

Cut two 2½" x 18½" strips for the inner border.

Cut two 2½" x 22½" strips for the inner border.

White: Cut three 2½" strips of white for the nine-patches.

Cut twenty 2" squares for the stars (2B).

Cut five 4¼" squares, then cut in half diagonally twice for the stars (1B).

Piecing and Pressing

Use ¼" seam allowance. Press the direction the arrows indicate.

SAWTOOTH STARS

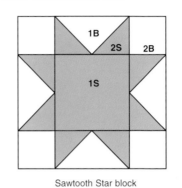

Sawtooth Star block

The ^ indicates what points to line up.

1. Sew a 2S triangle to each side of 1B triangle. Repeat three more times. Press.

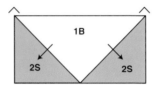

Stitch a 2S to each side of a 1B.

2. Arrange and sew the sawtooth stars as shown.

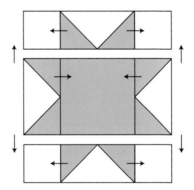

Arrange and sew the Sawtooth Star block.

3. Repeat Steps 1 and 2 until you have all five sawtooth stars sewn.

NINE-PATCHES

4. Set A: Sew a yellow strip to each long edge of a white strip. Press.

5. Cut set A into eight 2½" segments.

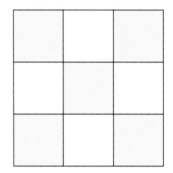

Nine-Patch block

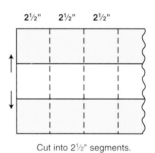

Cut into 2½" segments.

6. Set B: Sew a white strip to each long edge of a yellow strip. Press.

7. Cut set B into four 2½" segments.

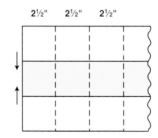

Cut into 2½" segments.

8. Arrange and sew sets A and B as shown into four nine-patches. Press.

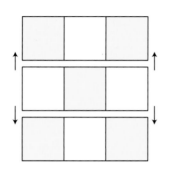

Arrange and sew the Nine-Patch blocks.

9. Lay out your sawtooth stars and nine-patches as shown. Note that they are in a straight set.

10. Sew the blocks into rows, press, and then sew the rows together. Press.

11. Sew the 18½" yellow inner borders to the sides and then the 22½" yellow inner borders to the top and bottom. Press.

12. Repeat with the blue outer borders, attaching the 22½" borders to the sides and the 28½" borders to the top and bottom. Press.

Easy as that! Now it's time to mark the top, layer, baste, and quilt.

Quilting design placement

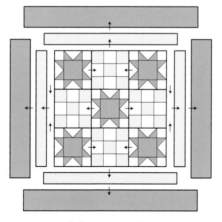

Quilt top construction

3 ALTERNATE COLOR SCHEMES

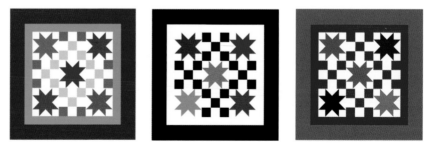

34

Join on dotted line.

Eight-
Pointed
Star

Join on dotted line.

Feathered Wreath

Segmented
Leaf

(rotate 180° to match quilt
on page 32)

Tulip

Flower

Basket

Single
Feather

Chain

Grape Leaf

Join on dotted line for
a complete pattern

Flip pattern along line ——→
for continuous border.

Flip pattern along this line at corner.

Grapevine

Join on dotted line for a
complete pattern ——→

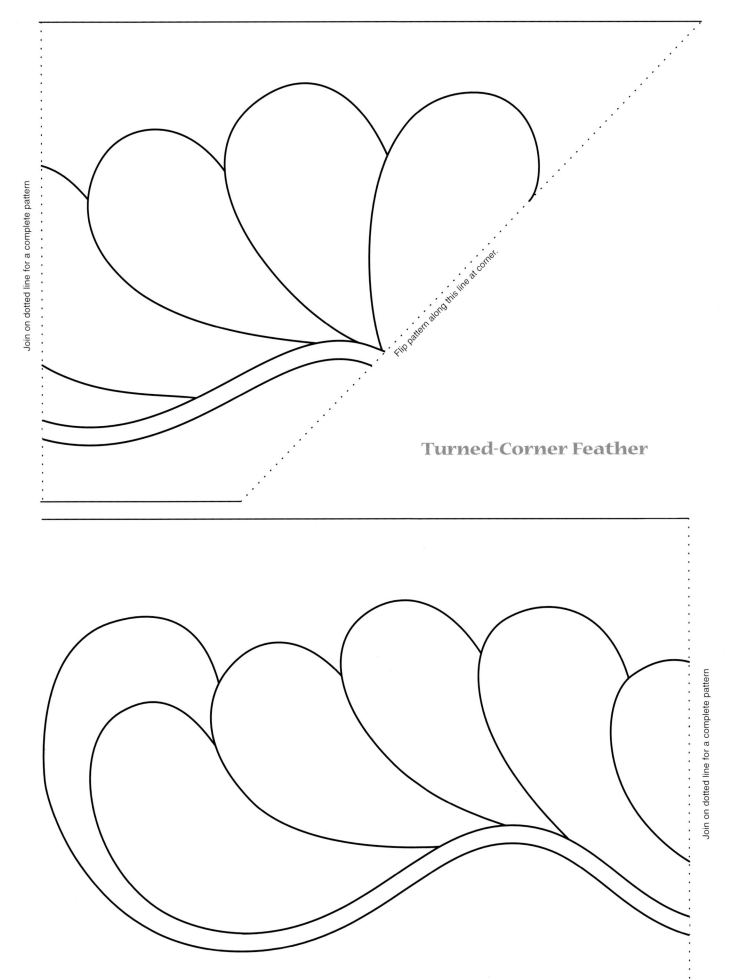

Join on dotted line for a complete pattern

Flip pattern along this line at corner.

Turned-Corner Feather

Join on dotted line for a complete pattern

Baptist Fans

Overlap patterns to create continuous borders.

Cable